TANISHQ:
Managing Turnaround

TANISHQ:
Managing Turnaround

PALAKH JAIN

PARTRIDGE
A Penguin Random House Company

ISBN: Softcover   978-1-4828-7147-0
               eBook   978-1-4828-7146-3

Print information available on the last page.

To order additional copies of this book, contact
Partridge India
000 800 10062 62
orders.india@partridgepublishing.com

www.partridgepublishing.com/india

INTRODUCTION

Indians, particularly women have been attracted to jewelry for centuries and this is reflected in the fact that Indians are world's second largest buyers of gold. The market for jewelry in the country is second only to that for food and the trade is built around so-called family jewelers - the relatively small, independent entities which operate through the large number of stand-alone establishments that are spread all over the country. The relationships with these jewelers are ones that are often generations old and is based largely on trust.

The Tanishq brand belongs to the Tata group and true to the group's policy; the brand aims at bringing in credibility and professionalism to the jewelry industry. India's jewelry market is estimated to be worth Rs. 60,000 crore a year. Of this the share of the organized sector - jewelry stores and brands managed by corporate houses - stands at only about 3-3.5% [6]. This small but significant niche is largely the creation of Tanishq. Today, Tanishq is recognized as a path-breaking effort that has earned a reputation for trust and excellence. It is credited for introducing pioneering concepts in an industry where tradition once ruled. The brand had sales of around 1200 crore last year and is gunning for 2000 crore this year [9].

But it wasn't such a happy story all along. Launched in 1996[4], Tanishq had to face several challenges concerning value proposition and positioning in the retail market and had incurred losses for three consecutive years. We intend to study what went wrong in Tanishq's entry strategy and how Tanishq has managed to turn itself around into a profit making entity.

THE ENTRY

B ack in the late 80s, the Tata group was having foreign exchange problems and decided to enter into the lucrative jewelry exports business to take care of these troubles on their own. Jewelry sounded as the ideal business opportunity because of India's large skill base and the low capital investment involved. Therefore they built a plant in Hosur, Tamil Nadu under the brand name of Titan Industries Ltd. (TIL). However, by the time it acquired the necessary skills and built the plant (1994), the global scenario had completely changed. Firstly, following liberalization in 1991, there was no longer any foreign exchange crisis as the country's balance of payments account had improved considerably. Also, the global demands had tapered off and with increased supply from India's Asian counterparts and the margins had become thinner.

Since the export option was no longer attractive enough, TIL decided to focus on the Indian market and launched the Tanishq brand in 1996.

MARKET SCENARIO

--- ⌘⌘ ---

The market for gold was characterized by the following features at that point in time:

High Consumption

Gold was a symbol of status for most Indian families and wearing it was a norm in gatherings such as weddings, formal events, parties etc. India was the second largest consumer of gold in the world after USA.

Highly Unorganized

Launching a brand in the Indian jewelry sector was an untried concept. The jewelry business in India was highly fragmented and ruled over by local players. There was no national jeweler that people could buy from, despite the fact that India was the second largest consumer of gold in the world. There were more than 300,000 independent, individual cities, though a few had expanded to acquire a state-wide presence. By and large, these stores offered non-branded jewelry retailers in India. The vast majority of these were singular entities that functioned out of conventional Indian designs and were difficult to pin down on quality. Establishing quality itself was a challenge since standards within the segment vary considerably. Hence the local jewelers had a very tight hold on their markets and it was difficult for a pan-Indian player to break into.

Unethical

Being ethical too was a problem as the market was riddled with unethical business practices like over stating the karat-age of gold, misrepresentation of quality and tax evasion. It is important to note that in spite of this, there was little insistence from the consumers for greater proof of the quality of gold used for making their jewelry. This is indicative of the extent of trust that the local jewelers enjoyed.

Lower restrictions

After liberalization in 1991, there was a considerable easing of restrictions related to import of gold. Before 1992, only the Metal and Mineral Trading Corporation and the State Bank of India were allowed to import gold. In 1992, as part of economic liberalization, the government abolished the Gold Control Act of

1962. This made way for free import of gold by any player. In 1993, the so far restricted gold and diamond mining industry was thrown open to private players. The situation was made even more encouraging by allowing foreign investors to hold up to 50% equity in mining ventures. [5]

Titan realized that there was a huge untapped market for branded jewelry in India itself. The critical success factors in the business were quality, fashionable design and good after-sales service. As a company which was part of the Tata group, known for maintaining high ethical standards, Tanishq prided itself on delivering customer value through a fair and transparent business model. But all of the groups efforts came to nothing as Tanishq was not able to break into Indian market and suffered losses for four consecutive years.

WHAT WENT WRONG: UNDERSTANDING THE MISTAKES

The key elements of Tanishq's entry strategy which went wrong are discussed:

Positioning

Tanishq tried to position itself as a premium brand which sold jewelry as a fashion accessory rather than an investment. The products offered by Tanishq were seen as elite and westernized. It was extremely difficult to convince the loyal Indian gold consumer of the change in the perception of jewelry from an asset to a fashion accessory.

People generally bought gold from the same family jeweler they had trusted implicitly for generations. Moreover, these jewelers made the jewelry to order and also offered the option of buying back their products at the prevailing market rates. Tanishq fell short on both these counts. Also, Tanishq offered only plain gold jewelry and thus ignored a major component of the market that bought studded jewelry.

Pricing

With the focus on pure jewelry, Tanishq positioned itself as a high premium brand meant for the rich and famous. It set the prices of its products accordingly which were out of reach for the middle class. The entry price barrier was very high. Thus the target market segment was such that the potential number of users was much lesser than the total Indian market for gold.

Also, the prices were not uniform across the country and there was no break up of price as charges for gold and charges for making. Thus consumers preferred the local jewelers who kept the making charges very low, even though the god that they offered was highly impure.

Designs

With its focus on exports, Tanishq's designs that were being introduced in India were conceptualized for the Western markets. Hence, the sleek and contemporary designs were meant to attract the European market. These designs were very different from the expectations and the tastes of the traditional Indian consumer who was used to heavy, traditional designs. This proved to be a major setback for Tanishq as the domestic consumer refused to purchase a westernized concept. Also, since gold jewelry is greatly in demand during weddings and other festive occasions, Tanishq missed out on this huge market due to its westernized designs.

Moreover, the company aimed to promote gold watches more than jewelry. This was an entirely different product offering and its promotion should have been carried out differently from the jewelry products.

Retailing Platform

Tanishq chose to sell its jewelry through shop-in-shop formats rather than setting up their own exclusive retail outlets. This proved to be a grave mistake as the decision put Tanishq offerings at par with thousands of other outlets selling jewelry. The brand missed out on an opportunity to differentiate itself. It also sent out confusing signals to customers who could not understand the rationale behind the high prices in the absence of any perceptible product differentiation.

18 Carat vs. 22 Carat

Tanishq offered the European designs which came only in 18 carats. This was not preferred and in extreme cases not acceptable by Indian customers. Customer surveys revealed that Indians bought gold jewelry for reasons related to the value associated with gold more often than the superiority of designs. The preference was for 22 and 24 carat gold which Tanishq did not provide.

Communication campaign

This was a key area where Tanishq's strategy went completely wrong. Although Tanishq positioned itself as the high premium brand, the advertising mediums (newspapers, magazines etc.) that it chose were completely out of sync with its image. The customers in the targeted high end segment were unimpressed by this lack of exclusivity and easy availability. This was one of the major factors due to which the brand received lukewarm response.

Mini Exodus

The company had its share of issues related to retaining talent. In May 2000, Xerxes Desai, the then managing director of the company had to face the difficult task of choosing his successor from between Bhaskar Bhat and Vasant Nangia. Bhat was the man chosen for the job and was appointed as the managing director by Desai himself. Nangia was to be assigned the role of the chief operating officer. [4]

This however was unacceptable to Nangia who saw himself as the hands-on man at Tanishq. He was associated with Tanishq for twenty years and had been a part of crucial decision making processes such as the expansion plans to increase the number of exclusive boutique outlets to 67 (from the then existing 30) and launching the all new range of accessories for men. Hence a day after Bhat was announced at the successor to Desai, Nangia quit. What was especially hurting was the fact that Nangia took along with him six senior executives of Titan. These ex-employees regrouped and formed a new company of branded jewelry, OyzterBay. The brand sells jewelry through retail outlets as well as through its' website and competes directly with Tanishq.

Supply Chain Management Issues

The supply chain faced serious issues that affected the profitability of the entire business. The most pressing problem was that of inventory. The inventory management is especially critical in a business like jewelry since designs are outdated fast and the inventory of old designs remains of little value. Tanishq had failed to manage its inventory satisfactorily. For example: the inventory was as high as $34 million when the total turnover was about $75 million [7]. An indicator of how poorly the inventory was managed is the fact that the finished goods inventory was close to 80 per cent of total inventory. From the company's perspective, the reasons for high inventory levels were the irregular and rare indenting of inventory and the lack of ownership of the finished goods inventory. What was more unacceptable was that in spite of high inventory levels, the lead time for fulfilling orders was large due to the improper categorization of goods and the poor assortment planning.

Competitive scenario

Analyzing the branded jewelry market using Porter's five forces, we can gauge the scenario and get a better idea of what is needed to succeed.

TAKING STOCK OF THE SITUATION: CONCEPTUALIZING A TURNAROUND

A player like Tanishq, when it is in the situation as described above, needs to address the areas in which it had made mistakes. The analysis must be done keeping in mind that when a player has been in the market for a long period (5 years in case of Tanishq) it forms an image which can be hard to break out of. The need for Tanishq was to reinvent itself and break the mould. The areas which Tanishq would have to work on were:

1. Positioning

2. Platforms

3. Communication

4. Operational issues

Of these, communication involved parameters such as communication of value proposition and the way the ad budget is utilized. Operational issues included activities like maintaining relevance to consumer demand and pricing correctly. These were issues at the front end and the consumer would quickly notice any changes here. Behind the scenes, production processes, inventory control etc would have a more direct bearing on the price which the consumer would bear. The platform used to retail the products is perhaps the single most important communication tool for any retailer. Hence this would also play an important role in the turnaround of the brand.

IMPLEMENTING THE TURNAROUND

Tanishq, although it had identified an existing unaddressed opportunity, had fumbled in execution. With the foreign exchange situation alleviating, Tanishq looked inwards and had realized correctly that the Indian jewelry market, if it could be exploited, presented an irresistible opportunity. The sales had been flagging due to a combination of bad positioning and bad communication. What was needed was a jumpstart which would increase the footfalls in the stores and communicate to the public about the benefits of their offering. This combined would translate into increased sales and that would trickle down to the bottom-line.

Jumpstart

An opportunity presented itself at Tanishq's 5th anniversary. A large event was planned with a high discount being offered coupled with intense media coverage and a focused ad campaign. Tanishq's earlier advertisements had a disadvantage because they failed to clearly communicate their offering to the customers. This time, Tanishq hit the bull's eye by putting pictures of some of its products and communicating the features of its offerings to the customers. Tanishq also introduced a new entry level range starting from Rs. 399 [4]. The result was an instant boost in traffic, which converted to sales slowly as Tanishq fixed its other flaws.

Retailing platform

Earlier Tanishq used to retail through multi brand platforms such as kitsch jewelry stores or other outlets, but then it realized that it was sending conflicting signals through its publicity campaign and through its retailing policy. The changes involved moving to an exclusive boutique format. There were 47 boutiques by the year 2001 and they were spread across major metros and some smaller cities. The smaller cities led the metros in terms of growth, clocking in a scorching 150% as compared to their 45%.

Larger voice

Tanishq moved from opportunistic ad spending on festivals and other occasions and formed a marketing plan. The ad spend was organized by category and medium and saw a

54% increase year on year for the period 1996 to 2001. There was significant customization for regions as the markets differed greatly in the way they had to be addressed. Moreover the shift was from focusing on the affordability to the overall value proposition with a stress on the quality, purity and reliability.

Designs

The main area in which Tanishq was lagging behind was in understanding the consumer psyche. Originally Tanishq had designs aimed at the export market and combined with its apparent pricing; it presented a formidable image with which the Indian consumer did not identify. To break this mould, Tanishq hired Indian designers to come up with around 3500 new designs. Individual boutiques were given the flexibility to choose and stock the designs it felt would sell best [5]. The flexibility in layout and choosing stocks showed results and all boutiques were stocking the best sellers and other hot sellers. Designs were continually refreshed with 10% of the lineup being phased out each quarter. This gave the stores a chance to rejuvenate themselves with new offerings and gave the brand a youthful vibe which is not normally associated with jewelry.

Purity

A major shortcoming was the composition of the original portfolio of mainly designs in 18 karat. Indian's viewed gold primarily as an investment medium and only after that did they gauge the ornamental value [3]. Therefore a higher level of purity was demanded and expected. With the introduction of 22 and 24 karat jewelry, this gap was filled. As with any investment, there has to be a high level of trust established and in this case it was already present with the local jewelers. To gain an entry, Tanishq had to either slowly establish trust over time or it had to expose the jewelers who actually and conveniently happened to be responsible of misleading the trusting consumers.

Head to head with local competitors

Any custom jewelry making involved two separate charges on account of raw materials and skilled labor. Traditional jewelers offered extremely low making charges as they skimmed off the gold and diluted the purity. Being from a house of strong ethics, Tanishq did not subscribe to such activities and was unable to offer competitive rates. Instead of resigning to fate, Tanishq went on the offensive. Purchasing x-ray machines costing upwards of Rs. 1 million, it labeled them as "Karat meters" and positioned them in its largest boutiques. It then launched a drive to establish the (purity or lack of it) of traditionally made jewelry and the results were shocking with a whopping 65%

of the jewelry measuring under the claimed purity with some cases of purity as low as 10%! Having shown to the public that it offered genuine quality, it further accentuated its proposition by offering a buy back policy (albeit with some caveats). The result was a gaining of trust with the consumers and business rose by 20-30%.

Cost competitiveness

The cost competitiveness was pursued under two separate heads. Supply chain and inventory excellence was pursued to increase inventory turnover and to prevent any stagnant stock piling up. On the other hand operational excellence by improved manufacturing processes was also undertaken. A traditional manufacturing unit lost 8-10% of the raw material during a production cycle; Tanishq`s production unit at Hosur brought this figure down to 2%. This enabled it to compete with local manufacturers and retailers who had overall lower overheads.

It also held a tight leash with all its boutiques. To control inventory, a concept of sludge stock was introduced. Designs which were slower moving were disposed off at a discount through the Tanishq value marts and Tanishq mobile platforms. Sludge stock older than 15 months was recycled. The boutiques were evaluated on a variety of parameters including the age of the boutique, its location etc. There were targets of inventory turnover and a penalty associated with a large quantity of sludge stock. The result was that slow moving items dropped from 18% to 12% of inventory.

Customer is king

Having pursued reforms in all areas, the area of customer satisfaction was addressed next. The many components to this were an affordable range, trust, etc and all this had to be measurable and linked to incentives to motivate the boutiques to act on it. So, Tanishq introduced an entry level pendant for Rs. 600 and offered a portfolio which was wider than the competitors addressing every price point. Return guarantees were offered to establish trust and to differentiate themselves from the local jewelers.

Uniform pricing

There were other initiatives which Tanishq wanted to pursue to consolidate the market which is mostly fragmented. One such initiative was the standardization of price across all its stores. Gold prices varied across the country depending on local factors such as demand etc. but Tanishq wanted to remove this anomaly and a link with gold prices on the London Metal Exchange was being contemplated.

Newer areas

Having actively addressed the retail segment, Tanishq also ended up opening a highly profitable segment in the form of corporate gifts. With the national fascination with gold, gold as prizes or as assured gifts were always attractive incentives. Being the only significant national player, Tanishq leveraged its position to gain contracts from major companies and this has since become a significant and steady source of income.

Other than newer segments, Tanishq also successfully split up the existing segment of plain old jewelry into functional sub segments. Traditionally this was done on the basis of the base material such as gold/silver etc and sometimes on the basis of the enhancements in the sense the kind of stones being used such as semi precious stones or diamond jewelry. Tanishq broke away from this practice and used consumer oriented segmentation. The division was in the form of utility for the consumer such as every day wear, 9 to 5 wear, evening wear and jewelry for special occasions.

Newer Collections

New lines were introduced which aimed at unaddressed niches. There were regular introduction of new "Collections" such as collection G, Solo etc. Some of them are mentioned below along with the segment they addressed [8].

Collection	Value proposition/Niche/ Unique design element
Collection G	Regular office wear, discreet and contemporary.
Aria	Traditional seven stone jewelry
Diva	Pearl and diamond combination
Hoopla	Diamond loops
Solo	Single solitaire diamonds

The major advantage of such sub segmentation is that the high growth sub segments can be addressed on a case by case basis and given more emphasis. The disadvantages include the risk of niche players stepping in, and the increased overheads involved in attending to as many areas.

Diversification

Tanishq, then growing at 40% in a segment which was registering growths around 5% [1], was eating up the unorganized sector and forcing them to get their act together. But as their growth would taper off to a more realistic pace, it will need to look at newer avenues for its next high momentum segment. There are no plans from the parent company, Tata Sons to diversify Tanishq beyond jewelry, so the areas are limited to jewelry and some fringes of allied fields. The major thrust will be towards domestic market penetration and entrance to foreign markets. Tanishq should replicate its modus operandi here to any new market it caters to. This will ensure that it gains credibility as a mainstream player rather than an import oriented provider of Indian jewelry.

"ALL THAT GLITTERS IS NOT GOLD": LESSONS LEARNT

Tanishq provides the ideal case of a large player entering a fragmented market and it goes ahead and illustrates the pitfalls of bad market entry strategies. We need to keep in mind the key strengths which Tanishq developed:

1. Localization

2. Cost competitiveness

3. Delivering value

4. Identification of gaps in the offering of current market leader(s)

THE WAY FORWARD

Having successfully precipitated a consolidation in the fragmented industry, Tanishq has conquered a 70% market share of the branded jewelry segment [1]. Having opened a lucrative segment, the competition has come flowing in from everywhere, including within (OyzterBay). As the pioneer who set up the market for branded jewelry, the brand now faces threat of competition from brands offering the entire range of designs in diamond – from exclusive to affordable designs. There are also newer materials such as platinum and rhodium and the threat from these offerings must not be under estimated given the sharp increase in gold prices of late.

The consumer who needed to be educated is now demanding and a high threshold is set for any new product line or design. Although Tanishq is leading the way, it is not a market which can be taken for granted. The focus now is on providing exceptional value and the highest quality to retain the existing customers and to increase penetration to sustain growth.

REFERENCES

1. Bhaskar, B. (2007). Delivering value by delivering desirable brands. Retrieved March 24, 2008 from

   www.titanworld.com/stores/watches/ pdfs/HSBCInvestorMeetAugust%20 07-Websiteverson.ppt

2. Faleiro, N. (2000). Jewelers to the nation. Retrieved March 22, 2008 from

   http://www.rediff.com/money/2000/ jun/26titan.htm

3. IBEF (2006). Gems and Jewelry. Retrieved March 23, 2008 from

   www.ibef.org/download/ibef_%20 jewellery_06.pdf

4. Ganpati, P. (2003). How Tanishq turned around. Retrieved March 23, 2008 from

   http://in.rediff.com/money/2003/jul/04tan.htm

5. ICMR Case Studies and Management Resources (2005). Tanishq- The Turnaround Story. Retrieved March 22, 2008 from

   http://www.icmrindia.org/free%20resources/casestudies/Tanishq%20The%20Turnaround%20Story1.htm

6. Jain, V. (2007). We'll not use celebrities for above-the-line promos. Retrieved March 22, 2008 from

   http://www.financialexpress.com/news/Well-not-use-celebrities-for-abovetheline-promos/69967/

7. Kannabiran G. and Bhaumik, S. (2005). Corporate turnaround through effective supply change management: The case of a leading jewelry manufacturer in India. *Supply Chain Management: An International Journal, Volume 10, No.5:340-348*

8. Superbrand Book (2004). Retrieved March 21, 2008 from

   http://www.superbrandsindia.com/images/ superbrands_book_2004/tanishq/tanishq. htm

9. Retrieved March 22, 2008 from

   http://www.tanishq.co.in/